DASH CAMERAS EXPLAINED

STREAMLINE INSURANCE CLAIMS, ENSURE 24/7 SURVEILLANCE, AND SECURE YOUR FLEET

Anshul Garg

Worldwide Published by
Pendown Press

PENDOWN PRESS LLP
An ISO 9001 & ISO 14001 Certified Co.,
Regd. Office: 3767A, Kanhaiya Nagar,
Tri Nagar, Delhi-110035
Ph.: 8130886000, 9650072927
E-mail: info@pendownpress.com
Branch Office: 1A/2A, 20, Hari Sadan, Ansari Road,
Daryaganj, New Delhi-110002
Ph.: 011-45794768
Website: PendownPress.com

Edition: 2024
Price: ₹ 399/-
ISBN: 978-93-6338-236-7

Layout and Cover Designed by Pendown Graphics Team
Printed and Bound in India by Thomson Press India Ltd.

To my parents, who instilled in me the values of compassion, kindness, and selflessness, inspiring me to strive for a life of purpose and service to others. Your guidance and love have shaped me into the person I am today. Thank you for showing me the power of noble works. I dedicate this book to you with love and gratitude.

TABLE OF CONTENTS

Preface

Driving can be stressful. Accidents happen. But what if you had a silent witness to protect you?

Our roads are filled with uncertainties, from unexpected weather conditions to erratic drivers. In a world where seconds can change everything, having a reliable witness can make all the difference. This is where dash cameras step in.

More than just a recording device, a dash cam is your silent guardian on the road. It captures every moment, providing irrefutable evidence in case of accidents, disputes, or even acts of vandalism. Whether you're a cautious driver seeking extra peace of mind or a fleet manager responsible for multiple vehicles, this book is your comprehensive guide.

We'll delve into the intricacies of dash cam technology, exploring features, benefits, and considerations to help you make an informed decision. From basic models to advanced systems, we'll unravel the complexities and empower you to choose the perfect dash cam for your needs.

Beyond safety, dash cams offer unexpected advantages. Imagine capturing breathtaking scenery, documenting road trips, or even using the footage for educational purposes. The possibilities are endless.

This book is your invitation to explore the world of dash cameras. Let's embark on this journey together, discovering how this technology can enhance your driving experience and bring you peace of mind.

Happy reading!

Anshul Garg

❖ ❖ ❖

Acknowledgements

Dear Readers,

I am grateful for the opportunity to share my experiences and insights with you. This book represents a compilation of years of experience, learning, and growth. I hope that the words within these pages inspire, inform, and resonate with each reader.

I am deeply grateful to the wonderful individuals who have played instrumental roles in shaping my journey and contributing to my achievements.

My wife, Juhi, you are not just my partner but the foundation of my strength. I couldn't have done this without your love and patience.

Kiana, my wonderful child, your laughter and joy infuse my days with purpose and motivation. You inspire me to reach for the stars.

My mentor, Akshar Yadav, your guidance and wisdom have shaped me into the person I am today. I owe much of my success to your invaluable mentorship.

I'm thankful to my friend Dinesh Verma, CEO of Pendown Press, and his team for their support and suggestions throughout the creative process.

To all mentioned and those not named, your contributions have been crucial to my journey. Together, we have built something extraordinary, and I look forward to the continued journey of growth and success with each one of you.

Thank you for being a part of this shared experience.

❖ ❖ ❖

Introduction

Do you love your car?

I'm sure you do—just like everyone else. You want to keep it safe, just as you would protect your own child. It's more than just transportation; it's your trusted companion on life's journeys. But have you given it the protection it deserves?

Let's think about it:

You might have taken your car to a local modifier who fiddled with the nuts and bolts of your prized possession. Or perhaps you visited a high-end accessories shop that burned a hole in your pocket. But in both cases, did you get a solution that you fully understand?

Now, the thoughts that come to people's minds are that the car dash camera is a useless product, only meant for beautifying the car. Moreover, why spend extra on something when we already have a fully loaded car?

But I'll tell you, that's wrong. And it's mandatory! How? Wait, wait! I'll explain everything. Meanwhile, grab a cup of coffee, and while you finish it, let me give you a quick introduction about myself and what I do. After that, we'll head on to a long drive. Sounds okay, right?

It's the most important asset that you can give yourself and your car. Only an experienced electronics expert can tell you what are the major and minor impacts that this device can have in your life. This book is your on demand consultant for you.

So, hello, My name is Anshul Garg. I am an Industry Expert in Smart Electronics Gadgets and the proud owner of the brand "AUSHA." My journey started around six years ago in the world of smart electronics, and since then, I have been dedicated to researching and guiding businesses in improving their knowledge to choose the right product, be it for their sales or personal use.

Today, I deal with over 300 next-generation products, and the Vehicle DASH CAMERA remains at the top of my list in terms of research and revenue generation. From private cars to government vehicles, defence high-security vehicles, heavy earth movers, and even various locomotives in high-tech power plants, dash cameras are everywhere. And this love for cars and related technologies motivated me to delve deeper into the field. Based on my experiences and learnings, I decided to write this book for all of you. So, here I am with this guide, full of insights and knowledge.

It's all about buying and selling a suitable dash camera for your car, even if you know nothing about electronics or are not familiar with the latest car accessories.

So, that was a short introduction about myself. In the upcoming chapters, I've provided more details. Oh! I forgot to ask—coffee's finished?

Great! It's time to start our long drive. Buckle up and let's go!

❖ ❖ ❖

Chapter

01

Road Safety Reality

Almost everyone in today's world either owns a car or travels in one at some point in their lives. We spend more than half of our lives on the road!

Now, if you know that you are completely safe on the road, you might be mistaken, my friend. The level of risk you face at every touchpoint on the road is significantly higher than that faced by a SKYDIVER.

Yes, this is a fact!

Your chances of dying in a motor vehicle crash are about one in 93 (or 1.075%). In contrast, the likelihood of dying during tandem skydiving is one in 500,000 (or 0.0002%).

Yet, tragically, many people take their own lives and the lives of others on the road for granted.

Car manufacturers have implemented numerous safety features to protect drivers and passengers. You can easily find tips online, such as:

- Carry Required Documents
- Use Relevant Safety Gears
- Follow the Speed Limits
- Maintain a Safe Distance
- Never Drink and Drive
- Maintain the Car
- Drive Car Smartly

These are some of the traditional methods that everybody knows and is taught in every driving school. But we live in the real world, and the real world presents REAL problems. In reality, these seven points are not covered fully by any driver in India. And on top of that, add rash driving and poor road conditions, and your road journey can be summed up in one word: **Chaotic**.

This is where the Dash Camera comes into picture. As you read this book, you will come across some ***WoW*** Facts that will change your perception completely towards this product. This book will assist you in choosing the right dash camera, ensuring your safety, and making your drives more secure and peaceful.

By the end, you'll be equipped to make informed decisions and empower your family's safety.

And you might be wondering how I know all this. My story has the answer......

❖ ❖ ❖

Chapter
02

My Story

"LEAP OF FAITH" These three words are engraved in my soul, and they are what I follow in life. I have had many twists and turns in life, but I have become better and better with each moment because every time, I took the Leap of Faith.

My family is based in Delhi, and my father ran a garment shop in Chandni Chowk since 1984. When I was graduating, I went there sometimes, but it did not appeal to me because I did not like the nature of work. I had a strong interest in electronics from the start, and I used to open and assemble anything and everything that came my way, like computers, pens, video games, radios, etc., etc. I was interested in science fiction and theft movies that had more technical aspects. Even my grandfather used to say that I would become an expert in the electronics industry in the future.

Not many people know that I worked as a software developer for a small company. I had shifts starting from 5 PM and ending at 3 AM. Though it was a learning phase, I worked for a mere salary of ₹8,000 per month even though I was an IT engineer. To be honest, it was a suffocating environment. Life was miserable; it felt like being in a pit. Then, one fine day, I decided to leave the job and take the Leap of Faith to start something of my own. It was back in 2012, and at 22 years of age, I had no idea how to approach things.

Next, I started garment manufacturing in Karol Bagh, Delhi. I named it "Future Creations," thinking that we would be focusing on designs of the future. Being from a world of computers and suddenly starting own apparels manufacturing had its own challenges. Switching from a job to my own business took a little time. Moreover, the designs we made did not appeal in the same way we had expected. Maybe we put our hardware designs on garments or designed them in an old-fashioned floppy disk style!

And lastly, the market worked on a credit basis. This was also a by-product of the designs and execution, resulting in pushy sales and long credit periods. In the span of the next 6 months, my routine was as follows:

Wake Up, Eat, Call Debtors, Answer Creditors, Sleep, Repeat... Repeat...

Fast forward 2 years, and the struggle continued. I had over 50 lakhs in credits in the market, 80% of which exceeded the timeline of 6 months. I could foresee some of these credits turning into bad debts, which was again disturbing to see. In short, I had gotten out of a pit and ended up in a bigger hole.

Then I realized that if I closed my business today, I would end up losing the money in the market and would have to pay the creditors out of my own pocket. It was a phase of life where I wished I had not left my job, especially when I saw people jumping to much higher packages while I was stuck, fearing that I had wasted 3 years of my life.

At that stage of life, I had slippers on my feet but high-end technology on my mind. The only passion in my life was reading about the technology I always craved.

My friends and family would call me whenever they got stuck with electronics or technology-related products. I started guiding people on what to gift in tech or what gadgets to include in their inventory. Whether it was gifting a phone to their girlfriends or buying a new TV for their homes, I provided them with the right choices. I always explained advantages and disadvantages of the products so they could make informed decisions. They used to call me a gadget freak.

Then I realized there was a significant big gap between the technologies available in the market and the actual requirements that could meet their needs fully. Technology was available, but people did not know how to choose the right one. One day, I had a car accident where the other party was at fault, but they were able to influence the police because their relative was a government official. With no proof, we were deemed culprits and had to pay a heavy compensation amount. That Day, I felt the need for technology in my car to counter such incidents.

I saw a ray of hope and quickly started to shift my mind towards electronics to ensure people could be saved from such harassment. I started with a beta model and tested it with a few customers. I started selling online and surprisingly started enjoying the work more as I connected with what I was selling. Many companies started approaching us for such solutions. That's when I realized there was a genuine need for safety and security gadgets, and I studied what was on the market. In the span of a year, I reduced my garment credits, and pivoted my business from a credit-only model to one with 90% advance payment.

India has a huge population, but awareness of electronics is only limited to a handful of cities across the country. Moreover, the word 'TECHNOLOGY' scares most Indians, but in reality, it can help you in your daily life more than anything else. Hence, there is a lot of scope to teach people how to make their lives easier and how to keep themselves safe.

That's when we started our own brand, AUSHA, and started working to make Indians SMART & SAFE. Today, I work with many top companies, individuals, and brands. We are proud suppliers of various products to the Indian Defense, with dash camera being our top product.

Once you read this book, you will have a clear idea of how valuable a dash camera is and what points to consider when buying one in the market. I have experience from hundreds of case studies where we were able to impact the lives of thousands of people through our learnings. Through these insights, I have addressed the unaddressed concerns of people and helped them become safe wherever they go.

❖ ❖ ❖

Chapter

03

Who Should Read This Book?

- **People Who Own a Car That Is Very Precious to Them:** A vehicle, whether big or small, is precious to a person, as it's often the first significant gift they give to themselves or their loved ones. And nowadays, gifts come at a high cost. So, why not keep it and yourself safe while enjoying multiple benefits from a single point? This book will help you choose the right "JEWEL" for your car that will not only beautify it but also keep both of you safe.

- **People Who Are in The Car Accessory Business:** This book will share with you some amazing insights that will make you an expert in your field. Many business owners learn these tricks through feedback from unsatisfied clients, which often results in lost business. We will ensure that you don't have to go through those painful phases and that you are prepared for any such incidents. You will be able to increase your conversions 3-4 times by gaining our expert knowledge, presented in a concise and clear manner.
- **People Who Run Taxi and Trucking Companies:** The biggest pain point for these companies is ensuring the safety of their goods and drivers. We have addressed these concerns comprehensively. With the solutions we provide, taxi and trucking companies will be able to breathe easy, knowing their goods are safe, and will be able to deliver better results to their customers.
- **Driving Schools:** The number of emerging drivers in India is huge, and it's crucial for both the driver and the learner to have a safe and secure ride. We will cover the important aspects that these companies are knowingly or unknowingly facing in their daily operations.
- **Schools and Colleges:** With more than 25 crore school-going children in India and over 4 crore students enrolled in colleges, it is crucial that the transportation and logistics systems are robust.

- **Indian Defense:** WE PROTECT THE PEOPLE WHO PROTECT US. With over 50 lakh personnel employed in Indian Defense services, including the Indian Army, Air Force, Navy, Police, and other agencies, it's essential that their safety is not compromised.
- **Construction Companies:** For those dealing with heavy construction vehicles.
- **Emergency Vehicles:** Vehicles used by law enforcement, fire departments, and medical services, including police cars, fire trucks, and ambulances.

The secrets I share in this book apply to all these fields, as well as a number of other logistics users across the country and the world. We have covered the finest details and work on them on a weekly basis. All my tips and secrets are compiled in this game-changing book, which can be used to finalize what is best for you, erasing all your confusions.

❖ ❖ ❖

Chapter

04

Why Need a Book for a Dash Camera?

Two questions naturally come to mind: What is a dash camera, and why do we need an entire book dedicated to this single product?

Let me answer the first question.

A dashboard camera, commonly known as a dashcam, is an onboard camera that continuously records the view through a vehicle's front windscreen and, in some cases, the rear or other windows. Also referred to as a car digital video recorder (car DVR), driving recorder, or event data recorder (EDR), this device is known by various names such as incident video recorder, car camera, dash camera, and dashboard camera. They are typically mounted on the windshield or dashboard of the car, hence the name "car dash camera." It's important not to confuse these with the Android screens offered by various companies; they are entirely different products with distinct functionalities.

Now, let's address the second question: Why do we need an entire book for a single product?

When you go to the market, you'll find a wide variety of dash cameras available. However, be cautious—most products on the market don't truly address the pain points of the customers. Many of these cameras are basic models that, despite their price tags, fail to automate your safety or resolve your specific concerns. As a result, people often end up purchasing the wrong product, or one that doesn't fully meet their needs.

Big Army Vehicles X Dash Camera = Pain

For instance, the biggest pain point of the Indian Army is that no dash cam company has been able to successfully install cameras in their large vehicles. Every company that installs cameras in their big trucks ends up doing makeshift work. The dealer sells the stock, takes the payment, and walks away. Later, the army personnel have to search the market for installations and proper solutions. This is due to a lack of knowledge and proper solutions in the market.

The Result: Wasted money, and still no effective solution.

Furthermore, Army personnel often lack awareness of the features and functionalities of the products they purchase. This gap in knowledge leads to inefficiencies and missed opportunities to enhance their operational safety.

Why This Book Matters?

This book is not just about selecting the right dash camera; it's about equipping you with the knowledge to make informed decisions. Dash cameras have proven to be invaluable in many situations, providing crucial evidence and enhancing vehicle safety. Yet, many vehicle owners still rely on outdated or suboptimal models that don't offer the full range of benefits. This book bridges that gap, offering insights into the best practices for choosing, installing, and utilizing dash cameras effectively.

So without further delay, let's dive into the dash camera's numerous advantages and how it can transform your approach to vehicle safety and security.

❖ ❖ ❖

Chapter

05

The Pains and The Gains

Did you know that in India, road accidents occur every minute, leading to thousands of fatalities and injuries each year? This staggering statistic highlights a critical concern: "Are we truly safe on the road?" The surge in accidents and road-related incidents brings to light the need for effective solutions to ensure safety and security while driving.

Let me address the pointwise pains of people and how the dash camera solves all these issues.

First, consider the most important fear anyone has:

- Are We Safe on The Road?
- What If Someone Jumps in Front Of My Car?

- What if suddenly road rage happens? How to protect myself from police?
- Are my kids safe with the driver for school?

- On-road harassment for money?
- On-road theft of mobile phones/valuable items?
- Fighting for parking spaces?
- Car thefts?

- Nighttime security while the car is parked?

The list of questions goes on and on. All these concerns have one common answer: **"The Dashboard Camera."**

Suppose you are traveling on the road and a pedestrian suddenly jumps in front of your car. Without a dash camera, you would have no proof that it wasn't your fault. In a country like India, it is often assumed that the larger vehicle is at fault by default. Therefore, having a recording device in your car is crucial. This is where the dash camera comes into play. It connects to your cigarette lighter port and starts recording when the car is turned on. It automatically records all movements onto the memory card inserted into the camera. If someone jumps in front of your car, everything will be recorded, and you can clearly determine who was at fault. Additionally, these recordings are admissible in Indian police and court proceedings as legal evidence.

Quick Fact: Dash cameras equipped with a G-sensor work like an airbag for your footage. In the event of a sudden incident, the G-sensor locks a 30-second video, ensuring it cannot be edited or deleted. This provides full-proof legal evidence.

Similarly, if you are a victim of road rage, theft, or other incidents, dash camera recordings can help you avoid significant losses by providing clear evidence.

You can see how dash cameras have led to the arrest of culprits and prevented further problems on the road.

Legal Implications and Insurance Claims

The second pain point for customers is the **Legal Implications and Insurance Claims** in the event of an accident. In addition to providing evidence in court, dash cams can also speed up the claim process by offering clear video evidence with date and time stamp to insurance companies. This can reduce reliance on statements and police reports, making the process more transparent and fair.

Installing a dash cam in your car can have a positive impact on your car insurance. In the event of an accident, having a dash cam can simplify the claims process. Dash cams provide indisputable proof of events, allowing the insurance claim to be more straightforward and ensuring that all parties are truthful. This can expedite the claims process and ensure that you receive the compensation you deserve.

Overall, dash cams are crucial tool for evidence collection and proving negligence in personal injury claims. They are powerful tools for preventing insurance fraud, ensuring safety, and protecting against liability. Dash cams can help drivers save money on insurance premiums, encourage safer driving habits, and provide valuable evidence in the event of an accident or criminal activity. Whether you are a fleet manager, commercial driver, or individual driver, investing in a dash cam is a smart decision that can benefit you in many ways.

Preventing Harassment and Fraud, Ensuring Safety

Real-Life Case Study

One time, my friend Chirag was traveling from Delhi to Gurugram. When he was trying to move from a traffic signal during a green light, it suddenly turned yellow while he was in the middle of the road. He was caught by the traffic police on the other side, who demanded a challan of ₹5000. Luckily, he had a dash camera installed in his car, which recorded the entire incident. He showed the recording to the policemen as a proof of his innocence, and they let him go. He later called to thank me, as I was the one who had insisted that he install the camera in his car.

Dash cams play a vital role in preventing insurance fraud, ensuring safety, and protecting against liability. They are essential tools for fleet management, commercial drivers, and individual drivers. Dash cams help eliminate "he-said-she-said" scenarios by providing concrete evidence to support the driver's account, ensuring a fair resolution and preventing false accusations.

One of the most significant benefits of dash cams is their ability to prevent fraudulent claims. Insurance fraud is a major issue that costs the insurance industry billions of dollars every year. Dash cams can deter fraudulent claims and reduce the number of false claims filed. When there is clear video evidence of an accident, insurers have a better chance of accurately determining fault and avoiding payment on illegitimate claims.

Dash cams also contribute to road safety. They capture footage of collisions, theft, vandalism, and staged accidents, providing valuable evidence that can be used to prosecute criminals and deter criminal activity. Additionally, dash cams encourage safer driving habits, as drivers know their actions are being recorded. This can lead to a reduction in accidents and a safer driving environment for all road users.

Moreover, dash cams can lead to discounts on insurance premiums. Many insurance companies offer discounts to drivers who use dash cams, as they are seen as valuable tools for reducing the frequency and severity of accidents. Studies have shown that some fleets experience up to an 86% decrease in accident-related costs when dash cams are used. Such a substantial difference is enough to encourage fleet management companies to equip all their vehicles with dash cameras.

❖ ❖ ❖

Chapter
06

Go Stress Free in Sleep

One of the standout features of modern dash cameras is **Parking Monitoring.** A parking monitoring dash cam uses sensors to monitor a parked car. It is a function that offers peace of mind even when your car is parked and turned off. This feature is particularly valuable for protecting your vehicle from potential damage or theft while you're away.

Parking Monitoring works by connecting the dash camera directly to your car's battery. This ensures that the camera remains powered and operational even when the vehicle is not running. If someone scratches, bumps, or tries to damage your car, you'll have a record of the incident, helping you identify the culprit and providing evidence for insurance claims or police reports.

Here are some key features of Parking Monitoring:

- **Parking Mode:** The camera records activity around your vehicle while the engine is off. It enters a low-power state, only activating when motion is detected, so it doesn't drain your battery.
- **Impact Detection:** Sensors in the camera detect any impact on the vehicle, capturing footage if the car is hit or bumped while parked.
- **Motion Detection:** If the external-facing cameras (front, rear, left, right, or interior) detect motion, they automatically start recording without alerting the intruder with flashing lights or screen activation. This footage can be accessed live or later.
- **Vibration Detection:** The camera's accelerometer senses vibrations and triggers recording if significant movement is detected.

With the dash camera, you can also record serene and beautiful car drives, which you can treasure in your memory box. This will capture beautiful memories that you would have otherwise been missed during your rides.

With parking monitoring, you can rest easy knowing that your vehicle is being watched over, even when you're not. This added layer of security not only helps protect your investment but also lets you sleep stress-free.

❖ ❖ ❖

Chapter

07

The Hidden Tool: G-Sensor

What is a G-Sensor in a Dash Cam?

A G-Sensor dash cam, also known as a Gravity Sensor, is a specialized feature equipped with an accelerometer. This sensor measures forces of acceleration, or 'G-forces', acting upon the vehicle. These forces could result from sudden changes in direction, braking, or impacts, such as during a collision.

The G-Sensor's primary function in a dash cam is to detect incidents **automatically.** When the G-Sensor detects a significant force, it triggers the dash cam to create and lock a 30-second video file. This locked file is then stored separately and is not overwritten when the storage is full, ensuring that critical footage is preserved for future review or as potential evidence.

In essence, a G-Sensor dash cam offers an additional layer of protection by automatically securing crucial video footage during unexpected or significant events on the road.

Real-Life Case Study

In one case, my client, Mr. Ramanjeet, purchased 100 dash cameras for his car rental company and installed them in all his cars. During a trip to Mumbai, one of his cars was hit from behind with such force that the axle broke on the spot. Thankfully, no one was injured in the incident, but the driver who hit the car insisted it was not his fault.

Ramanjeet knew about the G-Sensor very well, since we had trained him regarding it at the time of his purchasing the cameras. He knew that the recording of the incident would get locked on the spot and that it could be used later in court to settle disputes. He did the same and received very good compensation for the accident. He became a loyal friend and fan of our product, and has since referred multiple clients to us, generating numerous connections for us.

Benefits of a G-Sensor

A G-Sensor brings several key benefits to the table, enhancing overall road safety and security:

Automatic Incident Detection and Recording

The G-Sensor detects sudden changes in motion or impact, automatically triggering the dash cam to save the ongoing recording in a locked format. This feature provides crucial video evidence in the event of an accident, hit-and-run, or other incidents.

Incident Recorded with Sound

With an inbuilt microphone, the dash cam captures the driver's reaction, surrounding sounds during road rage, harassment, and other incidents.

Emergency Battery

In case the vehicle's electrical system is damaged during an incident, the dash cam will continue to function. It has an inbuilt emergency battery that allows it to record a 30-second video in such situations.

Overall, a G-Sensor dash cam offers drivers a smart and automated way to document crucial events that traditional dash cams might miss or overwrite.

How G-Sensor Dash Cams Work?

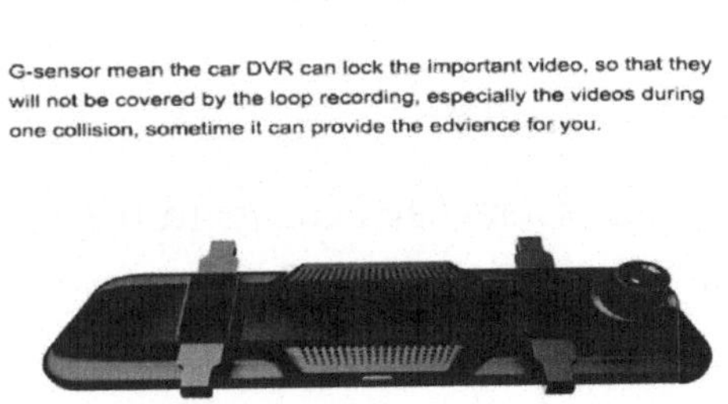

The G-Sensor in a dash cam operates based on the principles of acceleration. In simple terms, acceleration refers to any change in velocity — whether speeding up, slowing down, or changing direction. These changes cause shifts in 'G-forces,' which the sensor detects.

When the vehicle is moving normally, the forces acting on it are relatively constant, and the G-Sensor remains inactive. However, when there's a sudden change in movement — such as swerving, hard braking, or colliding with another vehicle or object — the G-forces change significantly. The G-Sensor detects this sharp change and reacts by sending a signal to the dash cam.

Upon receiving this signal, the dash cam immediately 'locks' the current footage, preventing it from being overwritten. This process happens within a fraction of a second, ensuring that the critical moments before, during, and after an incident are captured and preserved.

It's worth noting that the sensitivity of the G-Sensor can often be adjusted in the dash cam settings, allowing users to fine-tune the sensor to avoid false triggers and ensure it responds appropriately when needed.

Exploring the Features of G-Sensor Dash Cams

A G-Sensor dash cam offers several essential features that enhance its performance and usability:

Adjustable Sensitivity

Most G-Sensor dash cams allow you to adjust the sensitivity of the sensor. This customization helps avoid unnecessary triggers from minor movements or bumpy roads.

File Protection

The G-Sensor dash cam automatically locks video files when it detects a significant force, ensuring these crucial recordings aren't overwritten when the memory card fills up.

Event Tagging

Some G-Sensor dash cams include a feature to tag or highlight incidents in the recorded footage, making it easier to locate and review specific moments.

Parking Mode

Even when your vehicle is off, the G-Sensor remains vigilant. It can detect impacts or movements, triggering the dash cam to start recording instantly, offering round-the-clock protection.

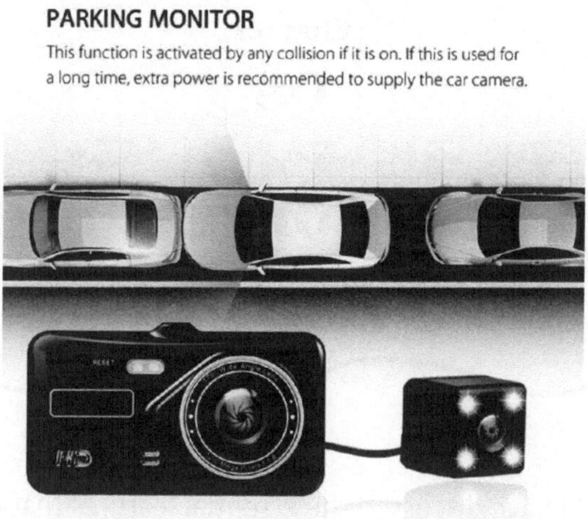

Shock Detection

G-Sensors can detect shocks or sudden movements, which is useful for capturing incidents like attempted vehicle break-ins or vandalism.

Conclusion

Think of a G-Sensor dash cam as your silent guardian on the road. It's there, quietly watching out for you, ready to capture those unexpected moments when things take a sudden turn. Whether you're dealing with a reckless driver or just want to keep an eye on your parked car, this tool makes sure you've got the proof you need when it matters most. It's like having an extra set of eyes that never blinks, keeping you covered in ways you might not even think about until you really need it.

❖ ❖ ❖

Chapter

08

A Step Toward The Next Generation

Until now, I have discussed the essential features that every dash camera should have before you buy one. However, there are also certain advanced-level features to consider before making a purchase. These features can enhance the functionality of your dash cam and potentially lower your insurance costs.

Let me show you a glimpse of those:

AI Technology

Advanced dash cams with built-in AI can detect issues like tailgating and distracted driving. This feature can alert you when a driver needs coaching on risky behavior and near misses before they escalate into problems that might affect insurance rates.

ADAS

ADAS stands for Advanced Driver Assistance Systems, which are electronic systems that use sensor technology to provide information, warnings, and assistance to drivers. ADAS primarily focuses on collision avoidance technologies and driver aids, enabling various levels of autonomous driving.

Real-Life Case Study

ADAS was a great help to my sister when she was learning to drive. Being a novice on Indian roads is a very difficult task since drivers don't always follow lane rules. The crowded roads make it difficult to predict where cars will come from. But with ADAS installed in my car, it helped her drive more confidently. ADAS alerted her if any car came too close or if a collision was imminent. ADAS is a technology that can do wonders for teaching new drivers and also enhance the experience for experienced drivers.

Night Vision

If you frequently drive at night, consider purchasing a dash cam with night vision capabilities. This feature uses infrared lights to capture clear footage in low-light conditions.

GPS

Some dash cams come equipped with GPS technology, which can track your location and speed. This information can be useful in the event of an accident, providing additional evidence to support your insurance claim.

High Definition

When shopping for a dash cam, look for one that offers high-definition video recording. A high-quality dash cam will capture clear footage that can be used as evidence in case of an accident.

Field of View

Consider the field of view of the dash cam you are considering. A wider field of view will capture more of the road and provide more comprehensive footage in the event of an accident.

Hardwired

Hardwiring your dash cam to your car's electrical system ensures that the camera will always be powered and recording. This eliminates the need to manually turn the camera on and off and is essential for setting up your Parking Monitoring system.

Smartphone Integration

Some dash cams offer smartphone integration, allowing you to view footage and adjust settings directly from your phone. You can view the live location of your car and see a live feed from anywhere in the world, which is convenient and easy to use.

360-Degree Dash Camera

Some dash cameras offer a 360-degree solution, allowing you to see all blind spots while driving. It is very useful when you turn the car left or right, as it shows you on the screen if there is any obstacle during the turn.

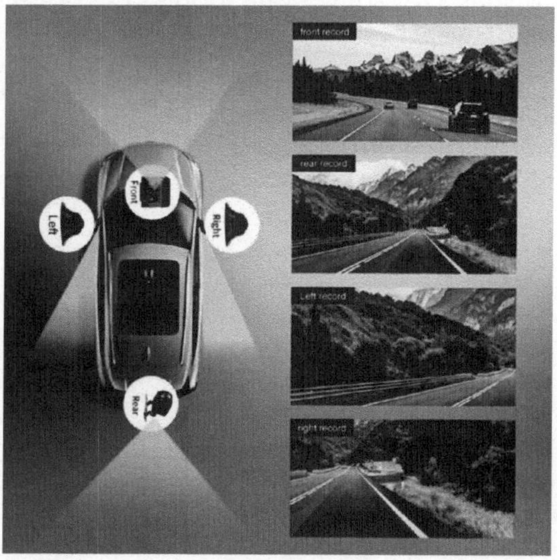

DMS

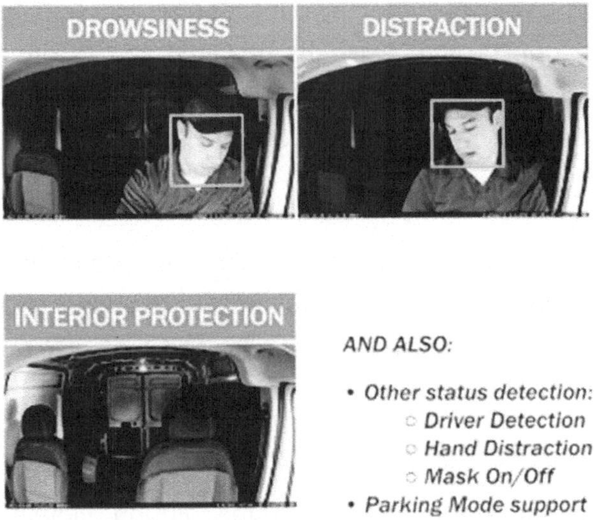

DMS stands for Driver Monitoring System, also known as the Driver Fatigue System. It is a camera pointed at the driver's face that provides a real-time evaluation of the driver's presence and state. If the driver is distracted, sleepy, smoking, or driving recklessly, the DMS will send out voice alerts to the driver as well as the central server. This system can help prevent a number of accidents.

❖ ❖ ❖

Bonus

The DO's and DO's to Follow

After all these valuable insights, many of you might have one last question in your mind:

"Will installing a dash camera void the warranty of my vehicle?"

The answer is **"NO."**

Dash cameras are external accessories that don't require any cutting of wires or undue modifications to the car. They simply need a 12-volt power source from the automobile's auxiliary power outlet, or in simpler terms, the cigarette lighter port. Even if hard wiring is required for parking monitoring, it will not affect the vehicle's warranty as it does not tamper with any of the vehicle's original fittings.

For those concerned about the installation process, it's straightforward and can be handled by a regular car mechanic. With just a brief 10-minute training session, most mechanics can efficiently install the dash camera, ensuring it is set up correctly and safely.

By following these guidelines, you can enjoy the numerous advantages of having a dash camera without worrying about affecting your vehicle's warranty.

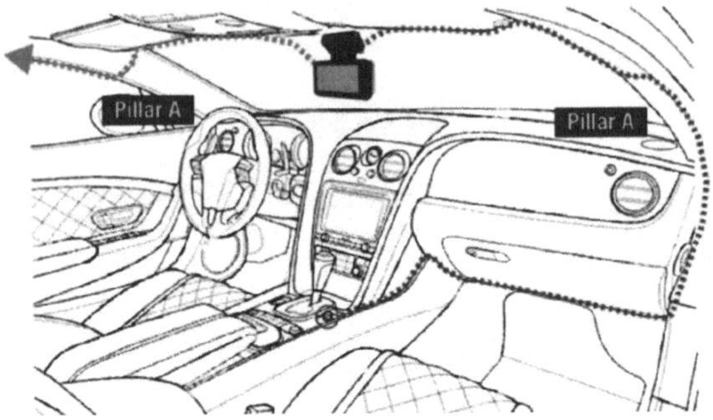
Pillar A
Pillar A

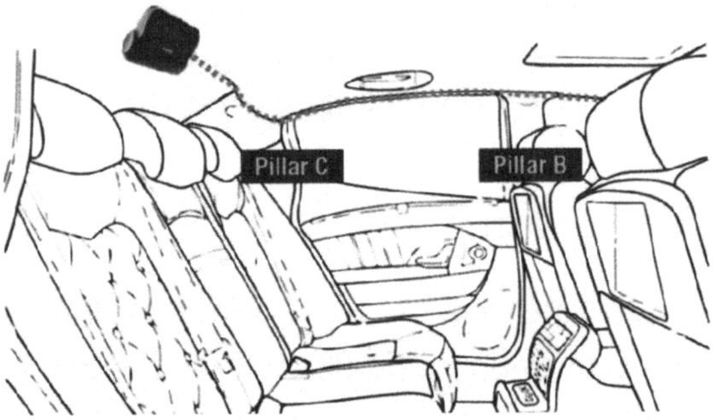
Pillar C
Pillar B

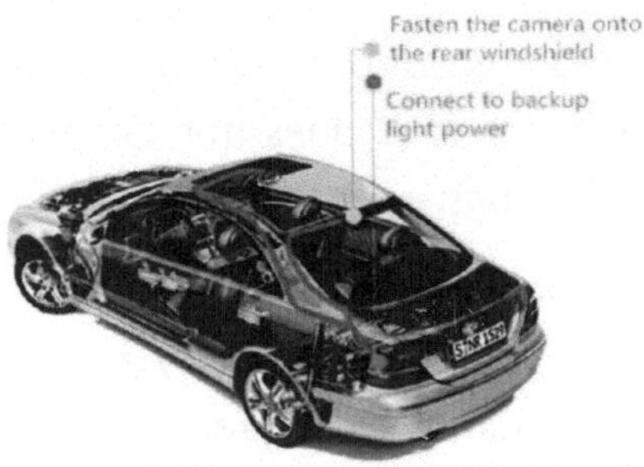
Fasten the camera onto the rear windshield
Connect to backup light power

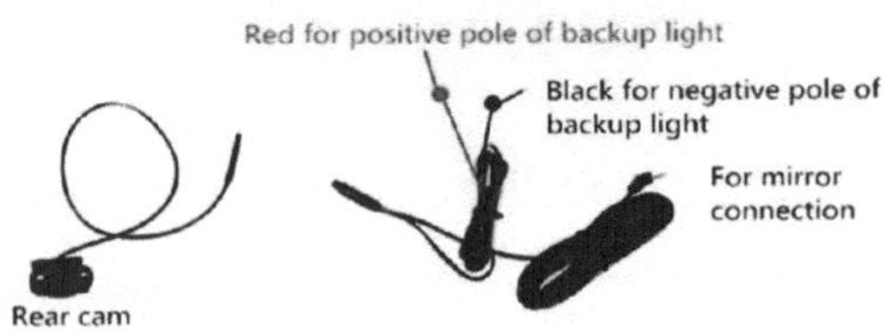
Red for positive pole of backup light
Black for negative pole of backup light
For mirror connection
Rear cam

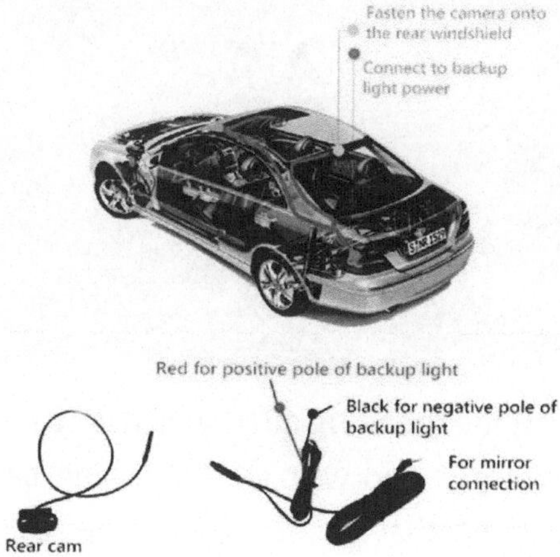

The installation is summed up in these images, and as you can see, it's that simple to install a dash camera in your car.

❖ ❖ ❖

Two Choices

Here we are, my friends, reaching the end of a beautiful and insightful journey! I hope you've enjoyed it.

Now that you understand the features and importance of a car dash camera, you are left with two choices.

- You can continue spending money on dash cameras without proper knowledge and wait for something bad to happen on the road. At that point, you might realize that you have bought a product that promised many things but fell agonizingly short.

Or

- You can have me by your side to help you make the right choice, ensuring that you and your vehicles remain safe.

The first choice leads you into a world full of scammers, where you'll always be uncertain if you've made the right decision.

The second is to have me by your side, ensuring a peaceful sleep and safe driving experience for you and your family. You have the full right to choose the right quality at the right price. The prices we offer start from a mere ₹1500 up to the premium range of ₹25, 000 rupees. And we suggest the suitable dash camera for you based on your exact needs.

I am a Smart Electronics Expert with the right knowledge, experience, and skills to help you stay safe in this unsafe world.

You can contact me at ***www.ausha.co.in***

or

reach me at: ***info@ausha.co.in.***

It's time to say goodbye. Oh, I almost forgot to ask—how was this long drive? Did you enjoy it? Please let me know by sending an email, and feel free to tell me if you'd like more such rides.

Looking forward to hearing from you soon!

Good Luck!

Wishing you a safe and sound life.

Anshul Garg

❖ ❖ ❖

Praises

We had a tough project on our hands that seemed very challenging. But once we joined hands with Anshul, it looked tough only on paper. He has been a constant guide and support, and I don't think things would have gone so smoothly without his expertise.

–Mr. Ram Galimelu

CFO - Johnnette Technologies

✍ ✍ ✍

What an amazing bundle of knowledge Anshul possesses! He doesn't see us as vendors but as growth partners. We can proudly say that we have gained an edge in the market and have been able to increase our revenue by at least 3X since we joined hands with him.

–Thamil Selvan

Deva System Solutions

✍ ✍ ✍

We would have kept switching between vendors for our dash cam requirements had we not found AUSHA and ANSHUL. The insights that he gave have helped avert some major accidents, and we have found a stable partner who is genuinely concerned for our safety rather than just selling the products.

–Wing Commander

Indian Air Force

✍ ✍ ✍

I came all the way from Noida to thank AUSHA and ANSHUL because it was their dash camera which saved me. A person jumped in front of my car to extort some money from me. The police arrived and were ready to file an FIR against me. At that moment, the dash camera video helped my case and proved that it wasn't my mistake. Highly RECOMMENDED!

–Sonu Gurnami

Dash Cam User

✍ ✍ ✍

How To Connect?

My brand Website: *www.ausha.co.in*

YouTube: *@AUSHAEXPORTSPVTLTD*

Instagram: *@aushaindia*

LinkedIn: *www.linkedin.com/in/anshul-garg-80b076231*

Facebook: *https://www.facebook.com/aushaexportpvtltd/*

Contact Details: *9873742793*

Address: *140, Sector 27, Gurgaon-122009 (Haryana), INDIA*

❖ ❖ ❖